Gracious Words

Joyce Eason

Contents

Chapter 1	Redemption From Transgressions
Chapter 2	Confession Leads to Forgiveness
Chapter 3	Tempted
Chapter 4	Praise
Chapter 5	Faith

Acknowledgement

This book is about the Gracious Words of our God spoken through His Son Jesus. God gave Jesus to us His creation to shed His blood for us for the penalty of sin which is death. Through Jesus' death to us Jesus gave to us the work of The Holy Spirit.

This book contains scripture from the Holy Bible.

The New King James Version Of The Bible.

This book is honor of my parents
Mrs. Cora Haughton Eason

&

Mr. John J. Eason

Also

To My Grandmother

Mrs. Rachel Everett Haughton

Chapter 1

Redemption From Transgressions

In this life we have transgressions that need the redemptive blood of Jesus to cleanse us from all unrighteousness. But that redemption can only come through the blood of Jesus. It's by God's Grace that we have that benefit which is better than any insurance. Allow these verses to minister to your spirit. In ministering we can have gracious words within our spirits.

"To the praise of the glory of His grace, which He freely bestowed on us in the Beloved. In Him we have redemption through His blood, the forgiveness of our trespasses, according to the riches of His grace."--Ephesians 1:6-7;

"Therefore if anyone is in Christ, he is a new creature; the old things passed away; behold, new things have come." --2 Corinthians 5:17;

"I will cleanse them from all their iniquity by which they have sinned against Me, and I will pardon all their iniquities by which they have sinned against Me and by which they have transgressed against Me." --Jeremiah 33:8;

"I, even I, am the one who wipes out your transgressions for My own sake, and I will not remember your sins." --Isaiah 43:25;

"Come now, and let us reason together,' says the LORD, 'Though your sins are as scarlet, they will be as white as snow; though they are red like crimson, they will be like wool.'" --Isaiah 1:18;

"As far as the east is from the west, So far has He removed our transgressions from us." --Psalm 103:12;

"The Lord is not slow about His promise, as some count slowness, but is patient toward you, not wishing for any to perish but for all to come to repentance." --2 Peter 3:9;

"Let the wicked forsake his way and the unrighteous man his thoughts; and let him return to the LORD, and He will have compassion on him, and to our God, for He will abundantly pardon."
--Isaiah 55:7;

"My little children, I am writing these things to you so that you may not sin. And if anyone sins, we have an Advocate with the Father, Jesus Christ the righteous"--1 John 2:1;

"When you were dead in your transgressions and the uncircumcision of your flesh, He made you alive together with Him, having forgiven us all our transgressions." --Colossians 2:13;

"How blessed is he whose transgression is forgiven, Whose sin is covered! How blessed is the man to whom the LORD does not impute iniquity, And in whose spirit there is no deceit!" --Psalm 32:1-2;

"Brethren, join in following my example, and observe those who walk according to the pattern you have in us." --Philippians 3:17;

"Now therefore, I pray You, if I have found favor in Your sight, let me know Your ways that I may know You, so that I may find favor in Your sight." --Exodus 33:13;

Chapter 2

Confession Leads To Forgiveness

Sometimes we have a hard time wanting to own up to being wrong. Then sometimes I find myself not wanting to admit when I'm wrong. The Holy Spirit's conviction causes me to look within myself with a Holy Spirit flash light of conviction then I confess my sins, shortcomings and wrongdoings to the Lord. Then I can have gracious words not to say ugly things about or to the people who treat me the worst but to keep gracious words in my spirit.

"Whenever you stand praying, forgive, if you have anything against anyone, so that your Father who is in heaven will also forgive you your transgressions." --Mark 11:25;

"So it is not the will of your Father who is in heaven that one of these little ones perish." --Matthew 18:14;

"And he will speak words to you by which you will be saved, you and all your household." --Acts 11:14;

"You are from God, little children, and have overcome them; because greater is He who is in you than he who is in the world." --1 John 4:4;

"If we confess our sins, He is faithful and righteous to forgive us our sins and to cleanse us from all unrighteousness." --1 John 1:9;

*"Then the Lord knows how to rescue the godly from temptation."
--2 Peter 2:9;*

"He who conceals his transgressions will not prosper, but he who confesses and forsakes them will find compassion." --Proverbs 28:13;

"For I will be merciful to their iniquities, and I will remember their sins no more." --Hebrews 8:12;

"Bearing with one another, and forgiving each other, whoever has a complaint against anyone; just as the Lord forgave you, so also should you." --Colossians 3:13;

But there is forgiveness with You, That You may be feared.
--Psalm 130:4;

To the Lord our God belong mercy and forgiveness, though we have rebelled against Him. --Daniel 9:9;

"And whenever you stand praying, if you have anything against anyone, forgive him, that your Father in heaven may also forgive you your trespasses.
--Mark 11:25;

I will deliver you from the Jewish people, as well as from the Gentiles, to whom I now send you, to open their eyes, in order to turn them from darkness to light, and from the power of Satan to God, that they may receive forgiveness of sins and an inheritance among those who are sanctified by faith in Me.'--Act 26:17-18;

In Him we have redemption through His blood, the forgiveness of sins, according to the riches of His grace.
-- Ephesians 1:7;

In whom we have redemption through His blood, the forgiveness of sins.
Colossians 1:14;

Chapter 3

Tempted

In this life we face temptations of all sorts but we must be strong not to let temptations draw us in to sin against God. Temptations can slip up on us. In order not to fall into the trap that the enemy sets we must continue to repent, pray without ceasing, meditate and read God's Holy Word the Bible. We must meditate on God's Word to keep His gracious Words in our hearts.

"Submit therefore to God. Resist the devil and he will flee from you."
--James 4:7;

"Let no one say when he is tempted, I am being tempted by God; for God cannot be tempted by evil, and He Himself does not tempt anyone. But each one is tempted when he is carried away and enticed by his own lust." --James 1:13, 14;

"For since He Himself was tempted in that which He has suffered, He is able to come to the aid of those who are tempted." --Hebrews 2:18;

"For sin shall not be master over you, for you are not under law but under grace." --Romans 6:14;

"Your word I have treasured in my heart, that I may not sin against You." --Psalms 119:11;

"Then the Lord knows how to rescue the godly from temptation and to reserve the unjust under punishment for the day of judgment, --2 Peter 2:9;

*"But examine everything carefully; hold fast to that which is good;
abstain from every form of evil."
--1 Thessalonians --5:21-22;*

No temptation has overtaken you except such as is common to man; but
God is faithful, who will not allow you to be tempted beyond what you are able, but with the temptation will also make the way of escape, that you may be able to bear it. --1 Corinthians 10:13;

"You shall not tempt the LORD your God as you tempted Him in Massah.
--Deuteronomy 6:16;

Brethren, if a man is overtaken in any trespass, you who are spiritual restore such a one in a spirit of gentleness, considering yourself lest you also be tempted. --Galatians 6:1;

For this reason, when I could no longer endure it, I sent to know your faith, lest by some means the tempter had tempted you, and our labor might be in vain. --1 Thessalonians 3:5;

For in that He Himself has suffered, being tempted, He is able to aid those who are tempted. --Hebrews 2:18;

For we do not have a High Priest who cannot sympathize with our weaknesses, but was in all points tempted as we are, yet without sin. --Hebrews 4:15;

They were stoned, they were sawn in two, were tempted, were slain with the sword. They wandered about in sheepskins and goatskins, being destitute, afflicted, tormented. --Hebrews 11:37;

Let no one say when he is tempted, "I am tempted by God"; for God cannot be tempted by evil, nor does He Himself tempt anyone.
--James 1:13;

But each one is tempted when he is drawn away by his own desires and enticed. James 1:14;

Chapter 4

Praise!

Praise is to applause God for being the Great Creator that He Is. We can have faith in Him that He is. Praise to me is another form of Worship because praise just allows us to give God His Tribute. God has done so much for me I can't tell it all. When I praise God I give honor and glory to the Most High honoring God through gracious Words which he has put in my heart.

*"To the praise of the glory of His grace, which He freely bestowed on
us in the Beloved. In Him we have redemption through His blood, the forgiveness of our trespasses, according to the riches of His grace."
--Ephesians 1:6-7;*

*"So that the proof of your faith, being more precious than gold which
is perishable, even though tested by fire, may be found to result in
praise and glory and honor at the revelation of Jesus Christ."
--1 Peter 1:7;*

*"For it is written, 'As I live, says the Lord, every knee shall bow to
Me, and every tongue shall give praise to God.'" --Romans 14:11;*

"Praise the Lord all you Gentiles, and let all the peoples praise Him."
--Romans 15:11;

"Saying, 'Amen, blessing and glory and wisdom and thanksgiving and honor and power and might, be to our God forever and ever. Amen.'"
--Revelation 7:12;

"Worthy is the Lamb that was slain to receive power and riches and wisdom and might and honor and glory and blessing."
--Revelation 5:12;

Praise the LORD! Praise God in His sanctuary; Praise Him in His mighty firmament! Praise Him for His mighty acts; Praise Him according to His excellent greatness! Praise Him with the sound of the trumpet; Praise Him with the lute and harp!--Psalm 150;1-3;

The LORD is my strength and song, And He has become my salvation; He is my God, and I will praise Him; My father's God, and I will exalt Him.--Exodus 15:2;

He is your praise, and He is your God, who has done for you these great and awesome things which your eyes have seen.-- Deuteronomy 10:21;

18) Also today the LORD has proclaimed you to be His special people, just as He promised you, that you should keep all His commandments, 19) and that He will set you high above all nations which He has made, in praise, in name, and in honor, and that you may be a holy people to the LORD your God, just as He has spoken."--Deuteronomy 26:18-19;

"Hear, O kings! Give ear, O princes! I, even I, will sing to the LORD; I will sing praise to the LORD God of Israel.--Judges 5:3;

I will call upon the LORD, who is worthy to be praised; So shall I be saved from my enemies.--2 Samuel 22:4;

Therefore I will give thanks to You, O LORD, among the Gentiles, And sing praises to Your name.--2 Samuel 22:50;

Now when the queen of Sheba heard of the fame of Solomon concerning the name of the LORD, she came to test him with hard questions.--1 Kings 10:1;

And he appointed some of the Levites to minister before the ark of the LORD, to commemorate, to thank, and to praise the LORD God of Israel:--1 Chronicles 16:4;

*For the L*ORD *is great and greatly to be praised; He is also to be feared above all gods. 1 Chronicles 16:25;*

And say, "Save us, O God of our salvation; Gather us together, and deliver us from the Gentiles, To give thanks to Your holy name, To triumph in Your praise."-- 1 Chronicles 16:35;

*Blessed be the L*ORD *God of Israel From everlasting to everlasting! And all the people said, "Amen!" and praised the L*ORD*. -- 1 Chronicles 16:36;*

"Now therefore, our God, We thank You And praise Your glorious name. --1 Chronicles 29:13;

11) And it came to pass when the priests came out of the Most Holy Place (for all the priests who were present had sanctified themselves, without keeping to their divisions),
12) and the Levites who were the singers, all those of Asaph and Heman and Jeduthun, with their sons and their brethren, stood at the east end of the altar, clothed in white linen, having cymbals, stringed instruments and harps, and with them one hundred and twenty priests sounding with trumpets

*13) indeed it came to pass, when the trumpeters and singers were as one, to make one sound to be heard in praising and thanking the LORD, and when they lifted up their voice with the trumpets and cymbals and instruments of music, and praised the LORD, saying: "For He is good, For His mercy endures forever," that the house, the house of the LORD, was filled with a cloud,
-- 2 Chronicles 5:11-13;*

*When all the children of Israel saw how the fire came down, and the glory of the LORD on the temple, they bowed their faces to the ground on the pavement, and worshiped and praised the LORD, saying: "For He is good, For His mercy endures forever."
--2 Chronicles 7:3;*

I will be glad and rejoice in You; I will sing praise to Your name, O Most High.--Psalm 9:2;

Sing praises to the LORD, who dwells in Zion! Declare His deeds among the people.--Psalm 9:11;

That I may tell of all Your praise In the gates of the daughter of Zion. I will rejoice in Your salvation.--Psalm 9:14;

I will call upon the LORD, who is worthy to be praised; So shall I be saved from my enemies.--Psalm 18:3;

*Therefore I will give thanks to You,
O LORD, among the Gentiles, And
sing praises to Your name.--Psalm 18:49;*

*Be exalted, O LORD, in Your own
strength! We will sing and praise Your
power.--Psalm 21:13;*

*You who fear the LORD, praise Him! All
you descendants of Jacob, glorify Him,
And fear Him, all you offspring of
Israel!--Psalm 22:23;*

*My praise shall be of You in the great
assembly; I will pay My vows before
those who fear Him.--Psalm 22:25;*

The poor shall eat and be satisfied; Those who seek Him will praise the LORD. Let your heart live forever!--Psalm 22:26;

And now my head shall be lifted up above my enemies all around me; Therefore I will offer sacrifices of joy in His tabernacle; I will sing, yes, I will sing praises to the LORD.-- Psalm 27:6;

The LORD is my strength and my shield; My heart trusted in Him, and I am helped; Therefore my heart greatly rejoices, And with my song I will praise Him.-- Psalm 28:7;

Give unto the LORD, O you mighty ones, Give unto the LORD glory and strength.--Psalm 29:1;

Sing praise to the LORD, you saints of His, And give thanks at the remembrance of His holy name.--Psalm 30:4;

"What profit is there in my blood, When I go down to the pit? Will the dust praise You? Will it declare Your truth?--Psalm 30:9;

To the end that my glory may sing praise to You and not be silent. O LORD my God, I will give thanks to You forever.--Psalm 30:12;

Rejoice in the LORD, O you righteous! For praise from the upright is beautiful.--Psalm 33:1;

Praise the LORD with the harp; Make melody to Him with an instrument of ten strings.--Psalm 33:2;

I will bless the LORD at all times; His praise shall continually be in my mouth.--Psalm 34:1;

I will give You thanks in the great assembly; I will praise You among many people.--Psalm 35:18;

And my tongue shall speak of Your righteousness And of Your praise all the day long.--Psalm 35:28;

He has put a new song in my mouth— Praise to our God; Many will see it and fear, And will trust in the LORD.--Psalm 40:3;

When I remember these things, I pour out my soul within me. For I used to go with the multitude; I went with them to the house of God, With the voice of joy and praise, With a multitude that kept a pilgrim feast.--Psalm 42:4;

*Why are you cast down, O my soul?
And why are you disquieted within me?
Hope in God, for I shall yet
praise Him For the help of His
countenance.--Psalm 42:5;*

*Why are you cast down, O my soul? And
why are you disquieted within me? Hope
in God; For I shall yet praise Him, The
help of my countenance and my God.--
Psalm 42:11;*

*Then I will go to the altar of God, To God
my exceeding joy; And on the harp I
will praise You, O God, my God.--4;*

Why are you cast down, O my soul? And why are you disquieted within me? Hope in God; For I shall yet praise Him, The help of my countenance and my God.— Psalm 43:5;

In God we boast all day long, And praise Your name forever. Selah .--Psalm 44:8;

I will make Your name to be remembered in all generations; Therefore the people shall praise You forever and ever. --Psalm 45:17;

Oh, clap your hands, all you peoples! Shout to God with the voice of triumph! --Psalm 47:1;

Sing praises to God, sing praises!
Sing praises to our King, sing praises!
--Psalm 47:6;

For God is the King of all the earth;
Sing praises with understanding.
--Psalm 47:7;

Great is the LORD, and greatly to be praised In the city of our God, In His holy mountain.--Psalm 48:1;

Let the peoples praise You, O God; Let all the peoples praise You.--Psalm 67:5;

Sing to God, you kingdoms of the earth; Oh, sing praises to the Lord, Selah
--Psalm 68:32;

Let heaven and earth praise Him, The seas and everything that moves in them.
--Psalm 69:34;

By You I have been upheld from birth; You are He who took me out of my mother's womb. My praise shall be continually of You. --Psalm 71:6;

And He shall live; And the gold of Sheba will be given to Him; Prayer also will be made for Him continually, And daily He shall be praised.--Psalm 72:15;

Oh, do not let the oppressed return ashamed! Let the poor and needy praise Your name.--Psalm 74:21;

But I will declare forever, I will sing praises to the God of Jacob. --Psalm 75:9;

Surely the wrath of man shall praise You; With the remainder of wrath You shall gird Yourself. --Psalm 76:10;

We will not hide them from their children, Telling to the generation to come the praises of the LORD, And His strength and His wonderful works that He has done.--Psalm 78:4;

So we, Your people and sheep of Your pasture, Will give You thanks forever; We will show forth Your praise to all generations.
--Psalm 79:13;

I will praise You, O Lord my God, with all my heart, And I will glorify Your name forevermore.--Psalm 86:12;

Will You work wonders for the dead? Shall the dead arise and praise You? Selah --Psalm 88:10;

And the heavens will praise Your wonders, O LORD; Your faithfulness also in the assembly of the saints.
–Psalm 89:5;

It is good to give thanks to the LORD, And to sing praises to Your name, O Most High;--Psalm92:1;

Oh, sing to the LORD a new song! Sing to the LORD, all the earth.--Psalm 96:1 ;

The LORD reigns; Let the earth rejoice; Let the multitude of isles be glad! --Psalm 97:1;

Oh, sing to the LORD a new song! For He has done marvelous things; His right hand and His holy arm have gained Him the victory.--Psalm 98:1 ;

*Shout joyfully to the L*ORD*, all the earth; Break forth in song, rejoice, and sing praises.--Psalm 98:4;*

Let them praise Your great and awesome name— He is holy.--Psalm 99:3;

*Make a joyful shout to the L*ORD*, all you lands!--Psalm 100:1 ;*

Enter into His gates with thanksgiving, And into His courts with praise. Be thankful to Him, and bless His name.--Psalm 100:4;

*I will sing of mercy and justice; To You, O L*ORD*, I will sing praises. –Psalm 101:1;*

This will be written for the generation to come, that a people yet to be created may praise the LORD. –Psalm 102:18;

Then they believed His words; They sang His praise. Psalm 106:12;

Save us, O LORD our God, And gather us from among the Gentiles, To give thanks to Your holy name, To triumph in Your praise.--Psalm 106:47;

Let them exalt Him also in the assembly of the people, And praise Him in the company of the elders.—Psalm 107:32;

O God, my heart is steadfast; I will sing and give praise, even with my glory.--Psalm 108:1;

I will praise You, O LORD, among the peoples, And I will sing praises to You among the nations.—Psalm 108:3;

Do not keep silent, O God of my praise! --Psalm 109:1;

I will greatly praise the LORD with my mouth; Yes, I will praise Him among the multitude.--Psalm 109:30;

Praise the LORD! I will praise the LORD with my whole heart, In the assembly of the upright and in the congregation.--Psalm 111:1;

Praise the LORD! Blessed is the man who fears the LORD, Who delights greatly in His commandments.--Psalm 112:1;

Praise the LORD! Praise, O servants of the LORD, Praise the name of the LORD! --Psalm 113:1 ;

From the rising of the sun to its going down The LORD's name is to be praised. --Psalm 113:3 ;

He grants the barren woman a home, Like a joyful mother of children. Praise the LORD!--Psalm 113:9;

The dead do not praise the LORD, Nor any who go down into silence.
--Psalm 115:17;

But we will bless the LORD From this time forth and
forevermore. Praise the LORD!
--Psalm 115:18;

In the courts of the LORD's house, In the midst of you, O
Jerusalem. Praise the LORD!
--Psalm 116:19;

Praise the LORD, all you Gentiles! Laud Him, all you peoples!   --Psalm 117:1 ;

For His merciful kindness is great toward us, And the truth of the LORD endures forever. Praise the LORD!--Psalm 117:2;

Oh, give thanks to the LORD, for He is good! For His mercy endures forever. --Psalm 118:1;

Open to me the gates of righteousness; I will go through them, And I will praise the LORD.--Psalm 118:19 ;

I will praise You, For You have answered me, And have become my salvation. --Psalm 118:21;

*You are my God, and I
will praise You; You are my God, I will
exalt You. Psalm 118:28;*

*I will praise You with uprightness of
heart, When I learn Your righteous
judgments.--Psalm 119:7;*

*Seven times a day I praise You, Because
of Your righteous judgments.
--Psalm 119:164;*

*My lips shall utter praise, For You teach
me Your statutes.
--Psalm 119:171;*

*Let my soul live, and it shall praise You;
And let Your judgments help me.
--Psalm 119:175;*

*Praise the LORD! Praise the name of
the LORD; Praise Him, O you servants of
the LORD!--Psalm 135:1;*

*Praise the LORD, for the LORD is good;
Sing praises to His name, for it
is pleasant.--Psalm 135:3;*

*All the kings of the earth
shall praise You, O LORD, When they
hear the words of Your mouth.
--Psalm 138:4;*

I will praise You, for I am fearfully and wonderfully made; Marvelous are Your works, And that my soul knows very well.—Psalm 139:14;--Psalm 142:7;

Bring my soul out of prison, That I may praise Your name; The righteous shall surround me, For You shall deal bountifully with me."--Psalm 142:7;

I will extol You, my God, O King; And I will bless Your name forever and ever --Psalm 145:1;

Praise Him for His mighty acts; Praise Him according to His excellent greatness!--Psalm 150:2;

Praise Him with the sound of the trumpet; Praise Him with the lute and harp.--Psalm 150:3;

Praise Him with the timbrel and dance; Praise Him with stringed instruments and flutes!--Psalm 150:4;

Praise Him with loud cymbals; Praise Him with clashing cymbals!--Psalm 150:5;

Let everything that has breath praise the LORD. Praise the LORD! --Psalm 150:6;

Let another man praise you, and not your own mouth; A stranger, and not your own lips.--Proverbs 27:2;

Those who forsake the law praise the wicked, But such as keep the law contend with them.--Proverbs 28:4;

Her children rise up and call her blessed; Her husband also, and he praises her:-- Proverbs 31:28;

Charm is deceitful and beauty is passing, But a woman who fears the LORD, she shall be praised.--Proverbs 31:30;

Give her of the fruit of her hands, And let her own works praise her in the gates.-- Proverbs 31:31;

And in that day you will say: "O LORD, I will praise You; Though You were angry with me, Your anger is turned away, and You comfort me. --Isaiah 12:1;

And in that day you will say:
"Praise the LORD, call upon His name;
Declare His deeds among the peoples,
Make mention that His name is exalted.
--Isaiah 12:4;

O LORD, You are my God. I will exalt You, I will praise Your name, For You have done
wonderful things; Your counsels of old are faithfulness and truth.
--Isaiah 25:1;

I am the LORD, that is My name; And My glory I will not give to another, Nor My praise to carved images.--Isaiah 42:8;

Sing to the LORD a new song, And His praise from the ends of the earth, You who go down to the sea, and all that is in it, You coastlands and you inhabitants of them!--Isaiah 42:10;

Let them give glory to the LORD, And declare His praise in the coastlands.--Isaiah 42:12;

*This people I have formed for Myself;
They shall declare My praise.
--Isaiah 43:21;*

*"For My name's sake I will defer My
anger, And for My praise I will restrain it
from you, So that I do not cut you off.
--Isaiah 48:9;*

*The multitude of camels shall cover
your land, The dromedaries of Midian
and Ephah; All those from Sheba shall
come; They shall bring gold and incense,
And they shall proclaim the praises of
the LORD.--Isaiah 60:6;*

Violence shall no longer be heard in your land, Neither wasting nor destruction within your borders; But you shall call your walls Salvation, And your gates Praise.—Isaiah 60:18;

To console those who mourn in Zion, To give them beauty for ashes, The oil of joy for mourning, The garment of praise for the spirit of heaviness; That they may be called trees of righteousness, The planting of the LORD, that He may be glorified."—Isaiah 61:3;

For as the earth brings forth its bud, As the garden causes the things that are sown in it to spring forth, So the Lord GOD will cause righteousness and praise to spring forth before all the nations.--Isaiah 61:11;

Heal me, O LORD, and I shall be healed; Save me, and I shall be saved, For You are my praise.--Jeremiah 17:14;

*And they shall come from the cities of Judah and from the places around Jerusalem, from the land of Benjamin and from the lowland, from the mountains and from the South, bringing burnt offerings and sacrifices, grain offerings and incense, bringing sacrifices of praise to the house of the LORD.
--Jeremiah 17:26;*

Sing to the LORD! Praise the LORD! For He has delivered the life of the poor from the hand of evildoers.--Jeremiah 20:13;

For thus says the LORD: "Sing with gladness for Jacob, And shout among the chief of the nations; Proclaim, give praise, and say, 'O LORD, save Your people, The remnant of Israel!'
--Jeremiah 31:7;

Then it shall be to Me a name of joy, a praise, and an honor before all nations of the earth, who shall hear all the good that I do to them; they shall fear and tremble for all the goodness and all the prosperity that I provide for it.'
--Jeremiah 33:9;

*the voice of joy and the voice of gladness,
the voice of the bridegroom and the voice
of the bride, the voice of those who will
say: "Praise the LORD of hosts, For
the LORD is good, For His
mercy endures forever"—and of
those who will bring the sacrifice
of praise into the house of the LORD. For
I will cause the captives of the land to
return as at the first,' says the LORD.
--Jeremiah 33:11;*

*No more praise of Moab. In Heshbon
they have devised evil against her:
'Come, and let us cut her off as a nation.'
You also shall be cut down, O Madmen!
The sword shall pursue you;
--Jeremiah 48:2;*

Why is the city of praise not deserted, the city of My joy? --Jeremiah 49:25;

"Oh, how Sheshach is taken! Oh, how the praise of the whole earth is seized! How Babylon has become desolate among the nations!--Jeremiah 51.41;

"I thank You and praise You, O God of my fathers; You have given me wisdom and might, And have now made known to me what we asked of You, For You have made known to us the king's demand." --Daniel 2:23;

Then Nebuchadnezzar went near the mouth of the burning fiery furnace and spoke, saying, "Shadrach, Meshach, and Abed-Nego, servants of the Most High God, come out, and come here." Then Shadrach, Meshach, and Abed-Nego came from the midst of the fire.--Daniel 3:26;

And at the end of the time I, Nebuchadnezzar, lifted my eyes to heaven, and my understanding returned to me; and I blessed the Most High and praised and honored Him who lives forever: For His dominion is an everlasting dominion, And His kingdom is from generation to generation.--Daniel 4:34;

Now I, Nebuchadnezzar, praise and extol and honor the King of heaven, all of whose works are truth, and His ways justice. And those who walk in pride He is able to put down.--Daniel 4:37;

They drank wine, and praised the gods of gold and silver, bronze and iron, wood and stone.--Daniel 5:4;

And you have lifted yourself up against the Lord of heaven. They have brought the vessels of His house before you, and you and your lords, your wives and your concubines, have drunk wine from them. And you have praised the gods of silver and gold, bronze and iron, wood and stone, which do not see or hear or know; and the God who holds your breath in His hand and owns all your ways, you have not glorified.--Daniel 5:23;

You shall eat in plenty and be satisfied, And praise the name of the L<small>ORD</small> your God, Who has dealt wondrously with you; And My people shall never be put to shame.--Joel 2:26;

*and said to Him, "Do You hear what these are saying?" And Jesus said to them, "Yes. Have you never read, 'Out of the mouth of babes and nursing infants You have perfected praise'?
--Matthew 21:16;*

And immediately he received his sight, and followed Him, glorifying God. And all the people, when they saw it, gave praise to God.--Luke 18:43;

Then, as He was now drawing near the descent of the Mount of Olives, the whole multitude of the disciples began to rejoice and praise God with a loud voice for all the mighty works they had seen,
--Luke 19:37;

for they loved the praise of men more than the praise of God. --John 12:43;

Chapter 5

Faith

Faith is beautiful because it opens up the supernatural voice speaking into the heart to believe that which is not scene. It causes us to speak into existence the impossible. It creates what God has birth in us to come out.

"Fixing our eyes on Jesus, the author and perfecter of faith, who for the joy set before Him endured the cross, despising the shame, and has sat down at the right hand of the throne of God."--Hebrews 12:2;

"For through the grace given to me I say to everyone among you not to think more highly of himself than he ought to think; but to think so as to have sound judgment, as God has allotted to each a measure of faith." --Romans 12:3;

"Now faith is the assurance of things hoped for, the conviction of things not seen." --Hebrews 11:1;

"For we walk by faith, not by sight."
--2 Corinthians 5:7;

"Faith comes from hearing, and hearing by the word of Christ." --Romans 10:17;

"The righteousness of God through faith in Jesus Christ for all those who believe; for there is no distinction; for all have sinned and fall short of the glory of God."--Romans 3:22-23;

"For in it the righteousness of God is revealed from faith to faith; as it is written, 'but the righteous man shall live by faith.'" --Romans 1:17;

5)"The apostles said to the Lord, 'Increase our faith!' And the Lord said,
6)'If you had faith like a mustard seed, you would say to this mulberry tree, "Be uprooted and be planted in the sea"; and it would obey you." --Luke 17:5-6;

"Though a host encamp against me, my heart will not fear; though war arise against me, in spite of this I shall be confident." --Psalm 27:3;

"Peace I leave with you; My peace I give to you; not as the world gives do I give to you. Do not let your heart be troubled, nor let it be fearful."
--John 14:27;

"Be strong and let your heart take courage, all you who hope in the LORD."--Psalm 31:24;

"In God I have put my trust, I shall not be afraid. What can man do to me?"--Psalm 56:11;

"In righteousness you will be established; you will be far from oppression, for you will not fear; and from terror, for it will not come near you."--Isaiah 54:14;

"Do not be afraid of sudden fear nor of the onslaught of the wicked when it comes; for the LORD will be your confidence and will keep your foot from being caught." --Proverbs 3:25-26;

*10) "No evil will befall you, nor will any plague come near your tent.
11) For He will give His angels charge concerning you, to guard you in all your ways." --Psalm 91:10-11;*

*"There is no fear in love; but perfect love casts out fear, because
fear involves punishment, and the one who fears is not perfected in love." --1 John 4:18;*

*"For you have not received a spirit of slavery leading to fear again,
but you have received a spirit of adoption as sons by which we cry out,
'Abba! Father!'" --Romans 8:15;*

"For God has not given us a spirit of timidity, but of power and love and discipline." --2 Timothy 1:7;

*"Now therefore, I pray You, if I have found favor in Your sight, let me know Your ways that I may know You, so that I may find favor in Your sight."
--Exodus 33:13;*

"Trust in the LORD with all your heart and do not lean on your own understanding. In all your ways acknowledge Him, and He will make your paths straight." --Proverbs 3:5-6;

"The LORD was going before them in a pillar of cloud by day to lead them on the way, and in a pillar of fire by night to give them light, that they might travel by day and by night."
--Exodus 13:21;

"I will instruct you and teach you in the way which you should go; I will counsel you with My eye upon you."
--Psalm 32:8;

"Lead me in Your truth and teach me, for You are the God of my salvation; for You I wait all the day."
--Psalm 25:5;

"O Lord, lead me in Your righteousness because of my foes; make Your way straight before me." --Psalm 5:8;

*"Faithful is He who calls you, and He also will bring it to pass."
--1 Thessalonians 5:24;*

"Train up a child in the way he should go, even when he is old he will not depart from it." --Proverbs 22:6;

*"Cast your burden upon the LORD and He will sustain you; He will never allow the righteous to be shaken."
--Psalm 55:22;*

"Who is among you that fears the LORD, that obeys the voice of His servant, that walks in darkness and has no light? Let him trust in the name of the LORD and rely on his God."
--Isaiah 50:10;

"So that the proof of your faith, being more precious than gold which is perishable, even though tested by fire, may be found to result in praise and glory and honor at the revelation of Jesus Christ."
--1 Peter 1:7;

Conclusion

I thank you for reading this book Gracious Words which has been in my heart for a while to write but finally I decided to sit down put scripture that has been dear to me on paper to share with an audience who desire to have a closer walk with Jesus.

The Books & Music of Joyce Eason

**The First Day Of The Rest Of My Life
Publisher Booksurge/Createspace 2010**

Music
Do You Remember? 2012
Publisher Createspace

**Dove & Sword Publications
To Know Why Then There Is No Why?
Publisher Createspace 2013**

**A Ring Of Bullies
Createspace 2013**

The Life History of Joyce Eason

Education
Amanda S. Cherry Elementary School
Activities: The Glee Club & Plays

Ahoskie High School
Activities: Bible Club, Historian Club

St. Augustine's College
Bachelor's Degree English
Studies: Spanish, French, Reading
NC State University
Advanced Spanish Courses

Activities: **1976-1980 Alpha Eta Omega Christian Fellowship and Concert Choir**, Offices: Assistant Secretary, Chaplain, Program Chairman,
Intervarsity Christian Fellowship
Joint Black Christian Fellowship/One of The Founders
Fulbright Participant 1977
English Club

Church Affiliations: Baptist, Holiness, Pentecostal
1972-1985 New Bethany Baptist Church Member
Vacation Bible School-Helper/Teacher

1972-1981 Zion Hill Baptist Church/Helper
Vacation Bible School, Sunday School, Bible School Teacher

1985-1989 Faith Temple Holiness Church Member
Activities: Choir, Church Typist, President Youth Choir, One of the Secretaries for Business Meeting,

1992-Present Soul Saving Station Church Member
Daycare 1995, Women's Conference Choir 1994-1999, Church Choir 1999-2001, Morning Prayer 2006-2007,
Book Committee, 2006-2007

Other Christian Affiliations

**Mt. Pleasant Bible Women's Fellowship
1986-present**

Church At Crossroads & Women's Christian Fellowship 2000-2007/2013-Present

**New Bethany Women Church Fellowship
2009-Present**

**Roanoke-Chowan Interstate Choir Guild
2009-2014**

Art Affiliations

Hertford Co. Arts Council 2013-Present